No Fear Nana!

Written by Tony Dallas
Illustrated by Lhaiza Morena

I am Moo Moo. My nana
visits me from Jamaica!

We go on a trip to town.
Nana has her ticket.

Nana sits and sighs.

6

Nana has no fear.

"Good morning, all," Nana grins.

This is good!

Look at this! This is good for you.

This is for you!

10

Look! This is for her hair!

And look at this, Moo Moo! I give this to you!

Going to town with Nana was fun!